Why shouldn't I eat junk food?

Kate Knighton

Illustrated by Adam Larkum

Designed by Nancy Leschnikoff

Edited by Jane Chisholm and Susan Meredith

Consultants: Simon Langley-Evans, Professor of Human Nutrition, University of Nottingham

Laura Stewart, Research Dietitian, University of Edinburgh

Contents

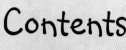
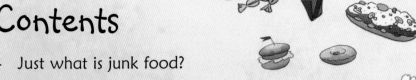

Just what is junk food?

Junk food is everywhere – in shops and supermarkets and fast-food restaurants. It's fairly cheap and lots of us love eating it. But what exactly is it?

Food scientists often disagree about what 'junk food' means. Some of them don't even recognize the term. But most would describe junk food as:

* food you get from many fast-food restaurants and takeaways, such as burgers, french fries, pastries, pies, pizza and doughnuts

* snack foods such as crisps, sweets, chocolate, some bought biscuits and cakes and fizzy drinks

* some of the processed food – food that has been made or put together in a factory – that you buy from the supermarket, such as frozen pizza and ready meals.

Most people agree that eating a lot of this kind of food isn't very good for you.

What makes it junk?

Junk food tends to be high in fat, sugar, salt and other things called additives. You can find out more about these later in the book. Everyone needs some fat, sugar and salt, but too much can be seriously unhealthy.
For example, sugar and fat give you energy, but if you combine too much energy with too little exercise it's fattening.

What your body needs to be healthy – and what junk food doesn't really have much of – is nutrients, or goodness. Nutrients are in fresh and natural foods, such as fruit, vegetables, beans, milk, cheese, eggs, fish and meat. Unfortunately, when food is processed, some of the goodness goes out of it and can sometimes be lost altogether.

What's wrong with eating it?

Nothing, as long as you only eat junk sometimes, and you eat a variety of healthier foods too. The problems only start when you eat too much. It can rot your teeth, make you pile on weight and generally make you unhealthy. After a while, it may even damage your heart.

What makes me eat it?

Lots of people eat junk food because it's
convenient. It's ready to eat straightaway,
or takes very little preparation and
cooking time. You can find it almost
everywhere and it's fairly cheap.
But, above all, most people think it
tastes pretty good.

Why does it taste so good?

The answer is simple – it's all the sugar, salt and fat.
Most people like the taste of sugar and salt. Everyone
needs a little salt in their diet, but many people add it
to food because they think it improves the taste.

Fat has a rich and smooth texture, which most people
like. Fat isn't just the white bit you can see on meat. It's
often in food, but you can't really see it, for example
like in margarine or cheese. The smell of cooking fat is
tempting too. And if you like the smell, it
excites the part of your brain that makes
you feel good. So a waft of french fries
alone could send you running into a fast-
food restaurant for a sneaky cheeseburger.

None of this means you have to eat these kinds of
food. Experts think that if you stop eating sweet or salty
foods, after a while you won't want them so much. And
you will probably find they taste too sweet or salty.

A quick fix

Another reason people often
reach for the junk is for a
quick energy boost. Fat and
sugar give you a lot of energy,
fast. Fat contains twice the
energy of most other kinds
of food, and sugar is easily
absorbed into your body.
This means you feel the effects
immediately. But, if you eat
too much of it and don't
exercise to burn off the
excess, it will build up as
body fat.

Added extras

Food companies know that people like salt, sugar and fat.
So they often add more than they need to, to make their
food more appealing. Sometimes, they add chemicals too,
to improve the look or the taste. These extras are known
as additives. You might not know they're in your food,
but the chances are you'll think they taste great.

Additives are often 'hidden' – difficult to spot on
packaging – so you have no idea of how unhealthy
the food may be. Food companies have to say what's
in the food they make, but the small print can often be
difficult to interpret. You can find out more about how
to understand it on pages 26-27.

What if I eat too much?

Eating junk food from time to time is okay, but too much can lead to trouble. You might notice that you're putting on weight, feeling out of breath, or getting spots. Some junk food may even make you feel restless, stop you sleeping or give you headaches.

And, if you eat junk most of the time, you may face more serious problems when you're older.

Terrible teeth

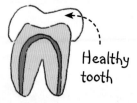

Healthy tooth

Food left on tooth

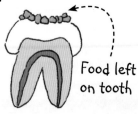

Hole in tooth

Most fizzy drinks and sweets are full of sugar that will cling to your teeth. The longer it clings there, the more damage it will do, slowly rotting your teeth so that you get holes in them.

Brushing your teeth twice a day is important – even more so if you've been eating sweets and drinking fizzy drinks.

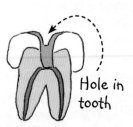

Fat attack

Your body uses fat to keep warm, build cells and to protect organs, such as your heart. But if you eat too much fat, it can make you overweight, or even obese. This makes you unfit – which means you will get out of breath easily when you do simple exercise like walking up the stairs.

Being unfit and overweight can make you feel tired, unhappy and lacking in confidence.

Different kinds of fat

Some fats are better for you than others. The fats in seeds, nuts, avocados and oily fish are really good for you. The fats in meat and dairy products, such as cheese, are called saturated fats and are fine in small quantities.

The worst kind of fat is known as hydrogenated fat and it's produced when making processed food. Too much of this could lead to heart disease when you're older.

What is heart disease?

If fat builds up, it can narrow the walls of your arteries – the tubes that carry blood around your body. This means that the blood can't flow very easily and oxygen doesn't reach important places, such as your brain. Sometimes fat causes a blockage in the blood flow, called a clot, which can trigger a heart attack. Other things can have this effect too, such as smoking or too much alcohol.

What's processed food?

All junk food is processed. This means it has been put together in a factory and the original ingredients have been changed in some way. But this doesn't mean that all processed food is junk — even a loaf of wholemeal bread has had to go through *some* processing.

All in the method

It's the way that food is processed that can make it junk. Processing foods at extremely high heat destroys nutrients, so there isn't much goodness left. And some of the additives put into food during processing can turn it into junk. Additives do lots of different jobs and have lots of different names. The list on the right shows you some of them.

What are additives?

Additives are natural or artificial chemicals added to food. They are added for lots of different reasons, some more useful than others. Some health experts think too many artificial additives are bad for you. This is partly because they take food further away from its natural form.

Additives used in food have to pass safety tests, so there is no real evidence that they're harmful, although some do have bad effects on certain people. For example, monosodium glutamate can give people a headache or stop them from sleeping. Other studies show that additives, especially those known as E numbers, can affect children's behaviour. No one can be sure what the long-term effects of all these additives will be, but new research is being carried out all the time.

Hidden additives

Stabilizing agents and **emulsifiers** are used to give food a smooth texture by blending fat into it.

Flavourings are added to give a certain taste to food. Chemical flavourings may taste like a particular food, but often don't actually contain anything of the natural product. For example, strawberry sweets probably won't have any real strawberries in them. But sometimes natural flavourings are added. Health experts think that these are better for you than chemical ones.

Sometimes **vitamins** and **minerals** are added to foods such as breakfast cereals. These are called **fortified foods** and are usually good for you.

Natural or artificial **colourings** are added to make food look better, so that you want to eat it.

Artificial **sweeteners,** such as aspartame, give food a sweeter taste without using sugar.

Preservatives help stop food from going off, so it stays safe to eat for longer. Lots of preservatives today are artificial, but food can also be preserved in natural things such as vinegar.

So what should I eat instead?

A good diet is all about balance
and variety – in other words,
eating the right amount of lots
of different foods.

Food groups

Dietitians divide food into the five groups shown below, so you
can see the kinds of things you should be eating and how much.

1. **Bread, potatoes, rice, pasta and cereals**
   These are starchy carbohydrates and you should eat lots, for energy.

2. **Fruit and vegetables (fresh, frozen or canned)**
   Eat at least five portions a day. These give you essential vitamins
   and minerals (see page 15), as well as fibre, which helps protect
   you from diseases. (Potatoes aren't included in this group.)

3. **Meat, fish, eggs, nuts, beans, lentils**
   Eat moderate amounts of these foods. They provide protein,
   which helps you to grow.

4. **Milk, cheese, yogurt**
   Eat moderate amounts. These foods contain calcium, which
   helps you to develop strong bones and teeth.

5. **Foods containing fat and/or sugar**
   Don't eat too many of these. Examples of foods that are
   mostly fat and sugar include cakes, ice cream and biscuits.

Helping you grow

It is even more important to eat a variety of foods during the time when you're growing up. Your body goes through changes and a good diet will help you cope with them all. You'll feel healthier and more energetic, and your hair and skin will look better too.

This chart shows what proportion of your food should come from each group. You should eat most from groups 1 and 2 and least from group 5, which is mostly junk foods.

Why do I need variety?

You need to eat foods from all five of the food groups on the previous page so that you can benefit from the different things they do for you.

Carbohydrates (groups 1 & 5)

Carbohydrates break down in your body and turn into a sugar called glucose which gives you energy. Starchy carbohydrates break down very slowly so that energy is released bit by bit and keeps you going for longer. It's better to eat the starchy carbohydrates from group 1 than the sugary, fatty foods from group 5.

Protein (groups 3 & 4)

Protein is the body-builder and repairer. For example, it makes the millions of new blood cells your body needs every minute. Protein is particularly important while you are still growing.

Fat (group 5)

Your body uses fat to keep you warm, to protect organs such as your kidneys and to help you absorb vitamins. Although it's good for you in small doses, too much can be dangerous.

Vitamins (especially group 2)

There are vitamins in all five food groups, but you get the most from fresh fruit and vegetables. Different vitamins do different jobs: some fight germs, some help you grow and others help your body to use the energy you get from food.

Iron, calcium & other minerals (groups 1-4)

Iron is good for your blood, and calcium gives you strong teeth and bones. These minerals are found in meat, leafy green vegetables, nuts, seeds and beans. Calcium is also found in dairy products. There are many other minerals too, in lots of different foods, but you only need tiny amounts of each one. If you eat a balanced diet, you should get them all.

Fibre (groups 1-3)

Fibre is found in vegetables, fruit, wholemeal bread and pasta, whole grain cereals, brown rice, beans and nuts. Fibre doesn't give you energy, but it is vital for keeping food moving through your body and preventing diseases. It helps make waste – or poo – soft enough to pass out of your body.

Try for five!

Eating five portions of fruit or vegetables a day may sound like a lot, but it's easier than you think. Sometimes it's confusing to know what and how much counts. These pages should give you a clearer idea.

What counts?

All fruit and vegetables count, whether they're fresh, frozen, chilled or canned. They all contain vitamins, minerals and fibre. A portion means roughly a handful.

You can eat as much fruit and veg as you like, but the bigger the variety of different types the better.

Smoothies

Smoothies are a great way to eat several portions of fruit at once. They're easiest to make if you have an electric blender. But, if not, mash soft fruits with a fork and mix in milk or fruit juice.

Berry delicious
(one serving)

100g mixed berries, such as
    blueberries, raspberries
    and strawberries

250ml (8½ fl oz) apple or
    orange juice

The great thing is, you don't always have to follow a recipe. Just experiment by throwing in all the things you like.

Soups

Soups are easy to make. They're also a delicious way to get a variety of vegetables in one dish. Chop up your vegetables into small pieces. Put them in a saucepan and just cover them with water. Simmer everything gently until the vegetables are cooked. You can keep the soup chunky or put it through a blender. Here are some scrumptious combinations...

* Leek and potato
* Red pepper and carrot
* Bacon, bean and lentil
* Sweet potato and parsnip
* Tomato and basil

The story of a chicken nugget

If you think chicken nuggets are made from succulent pieces of chicken breast rolled in fresh golden breadcrumbs, think again. Chicken nuggets are amongst the most highly processed and unhealthy foods you can buy.

Meat or skin?

Some of the worst chicken nuggets contain less than 30% chicken meat. This 30% may not even be the parts of the chicken you would think of, or hope for, such as breast, legs, wings and thighs. Nugget manufacturers often use chicken skin. Skin doesn't sound very appetizing and it's also extremely fattening. The manufacturers say that some skin is needed to bind nuggets together, but lots of nuggets have been found to contain more skin than anything else. The most likely reason for this is that skin is cheap.

The other 70%

So if only 30% is meat, what on earth is the rest of the nugget made up of? Some nuggets contain more than 40 separate ingredients, including water, pork fat, a starchy substance called rusk, wheat starch, sweeteners, hydrogenated vegetable oil, colourings and flavourings.

How do they get all that in?

Here's how to make a really unhealthy nugget...

1. Throw the various parts of the chicken, with some water, into a huge blender and blend until it is an unrecognizable paste.

2. Mix in some rusk and wheat starch to bulk it out. Then add as many chemical sweeteners and flavourings as you like.

3. Chuck in some sodium phosphate, to make it stick together, and lots of pork fat to keep it juicy.

4. Stir in another unhealthy fat, such as hydrogenated soybean oil. Mould the mixture into a nugget shape.

5. Coat the nugget in flour and more chemical flavourings and colourings, such as sodium acid pyrophosphate.

6. Finish the process by deep frying the nugget in hydrogenated vegetable oil.

Why not use 100% chicken?

Meat is expensive, and food companies find they can sell just as many nuggets by making them cheaply, stuffed with water, carbohydrates and chemicals instead.

You can buy good quality nuggets, though. But remember to check the ingredients to find out exactly what they're made up of. If you really like chicken nuggets and other junk food, you could make your own version. Over the page you'll find a healthy burger recipe.

It doesn't have to be junk

Burgers and nuggets don't have to be unhealthy. It all depends what they're made from and what you eat with them.

Burger meal 1

The burger in a typical fast-food restaurant meal contains up to 25g of fat, the french fries contain 23g and the milkshake 14g. That's almost all the fat you should eat in a day, in just one meal.

This milkshake has loads of sugar as well as fat.

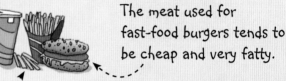

The meat used for fast-food burgers tends to be cheap and very fatty.

Because these fries are so thin and long, there is a large surface area to absorb fat. If they were chunkier, less of the potato would come into contact with fat.

Burger meal 2

A home-made burger meal could contain a total of only 15g of fat.

Fruit juice packed with vitamin C.

Home-made burger in a whole grain bread bun. Find out how to make the burger on the opposite page.

Potato wedges with their skins on baked in the oven with olive oil. (This is better to cook with than sunflower or vegetable oil, and the potato skins contain lots of nutrients too.)

If you make your own version of a 'junk' meal, you know exactly what has gone into it and you can be sure there are no unnecessary additives.

Make healthy burgers

This recipe serves 4

Ingredients:

2 slices of wholemeal bread

1 teaspoon dried mixed herbs

4 tablespoons milk

1 small red onion

450g (1lb) lean minced beef

salt and pepper

1 teaspoon olive oil

1. Heat the oven to 200°C (400°F, gas mark 6).

2. Trim the crusts off the bread and tear the bread into pieces. Put it in a bowl with the herbs and milk.

3. Leave the bread to soak for 2-3 minutes, then mash it with a fork. Peel and chop the onion finely, then add it.

4. Add the minced beef and a pinch of salt and pepper. Break up the beef with a wooden spoon, then, with clean hands, mix all the ingredients together.

5. Divide the mixture into four pieces. Press into burger shapes about 1cm (½ inch) thick.

6. Wipe the oil over a baking tray with a paper towel. Then, put the burgers on the tray.

7. Cook the burgers in the oven for 10 minutes. Then, lift the tray out, wearing oven gloves. Turn the burgers over and cook them for another 10 minutes.

8. Serve the burgers in toasted whole grain burger buns, with lettuce leaves and sliced tomatoes.

Why bother with breakfast?

You use some energy even when you're asleep, so when you wake up you need to recharge. Your body is hungry in the mornings, even if you don't feel it.

I can't lift my pencil.

People who don't eat breakfast feel more tired and sluggish during the morning.

Tests by scientists have shown that children who eat breakfast do better at school. Breakfasts that contains whole grains, fibre, calcium and protein boost your concentration and memory, and help you to learn. Some studies have even shown that students who eat breakfast have fewer absences from school.

If you don't have breakfast, you will be more likely to snack on sugary junk food for an energy boost.

Some people skip breakfast because they think it will help them lose weight. But research shows that having breakfast actually helps you stay at a healthy weight.

What's a healthy breakfast?

A good breakfast can provide up to a quarter of the nutrients and energy you need for the day. Here are some ideas:

Fruit juice

Cereal

Boiled egg and soldiers

A piece of fruit

Bread with jam or peanut butter

Scrambled egg on toast   Muesli and yogurt

A not-so-healthy breakfast

* Fried bacon, eggs, tomatoes and sausages
* Cereal with added salt, sugar or chocolate
* Cereal bars with added sugar
* Doughnuts and pastries
* A packet of crisps

A healthier version of a fry-up is to grill the bacon, sausages and tomatoes, and poach or scramble your eggs.

Break-time snack attack!

Everyone's peckish by break time, especially anyone who hasn't had breakfast. But instead of reaching for a bag of crisps or a chocolate bar, try a box of raisins or a piece of fruit. There are more snack ideas on pages 33 and 46.

School lunches

At school, you are often free to choose what you want to eat. But are you making the best choices?

An ideal lunch should contain carbohydrates, protein, fruit and vegetables, and be low in fat, sugar and salt. Experts think that eating junk for lunch can make you feel restless and unable to concentrate on your work. Not eating *enough* at lunchtime can make you feel the same way too.

School meals

In some schools junk food is easy to get hold of and hard to resist. But governments in many countries are working hard to try to improve school meals. They are worried about children becoming very overweight or obese and ill through a bad diet.

It's okay to eat burgers and chips sometimes, but try to choose from the healthier things that are on offer too.

You could choose a baked potato, pasta or rice dish, and always have at least one portion of vegetables or salad too. It's fine to have a chocolate pudding as a treat, but stick to a piece of fruit or yogurt most of the time. Try to drink pure unsweetened fruit juice or water instead of a fizzy drink.

Packed lunches

You can put almost anything in your lunchbox. For example, you could take healthy leftovers instead of a sandwich.

If you like sandwiches, make them from wholemeal bread instead of white, which doesn't contain as much goodness. Your lunchbox will be more interesting, and nutritionally varied, if you keep changing the menu...

Vary the type of bread
* Sliced, roll, baguette
* Bagels
* Pitta pockets
* Tortilla wraps

...and the fillings
* Avocado, bacon and cream cheese
* Cold sausage and tomato
* Beef and lettuce
* Tuna, egg and olives
* Salami, mozzarella and cherry tomatoes
* Tandoori chicken
* Feta cheese and cucumber
* Peanut butter and banana
* Cheese and apple
* Hummus and red pepper

Try a cold salad
* Pasta salad with pesto, cherry tomatoes and thinly sliced courgette
* Potato salad with cottage cheese, pineapple and ham
* Rice salad with uncooked mushrooms and sweetcorn, sultanas and spring onions

Add fruit and a low-fat yogurt too. For other healthy lunchbox ideas, see pages 33.

Tip: If you freeze your drink, it will keep the rest of your lunchbox chilled, until it defrosts in time for lunch.

What do the labels mean?

It can be hard to figure out if a food is healthy or not, and looking at the information on the packaging can be confusing.

Most packaged food has a label a bit like the one below. Look at the page opposite to find out what it all means.

NUTRITION INFORMATION	Chocolate digestive biscuits	
Average values	Per biscuit	Per 100g
ENERGY (kj) (kcal)	353 84	2039 487
PROTEIN	1.2g	6.7g
CARBOHYDRATE of which SUGARS	10.8g 5.1g	62.5g 29.3g
FAT of which SATURATES	4.0g 2.1g	23.3g 12.0g
FIBRE	0.5g	2.9g
SODIUM* *EQUIVALENT AS SALT	0.1g 0.25g	0.5g 1.25g

How much are you eating?

Food companies and supermarkets are trying to make labels clearer. Some put nutritional information on the front of the package, so that you can see it straightaway. It can be shown in different ways.

Many show you the amount of something, such as sugar, that the product contains and what percentage this is of your guideline daily amount (GDA) – the recommended amount you should eat of something each day.

The amounts are given per item or portion, or how much there is per 100 grams. Sometimes it may give you both.

Sometimes sugar is counted as part of the carbohydrates, as on this label. The 'of which SUGARS' part is the bit that you count as your sugar intake.

Sugar can have lots of different names, though, so look out for sucrose, fructose, glucose, maltose, honey, invert sugar and corn syrup.

The energy food gives you is measured in kilojoules (kj) or kilocalories (kcal). Girls need about 1600-2000 kilocalories a day and boys need around 1800-2000.

There are different kinds of fats (see page 9). The saturated part of the FAT here is the most unhealthy, so look at that amount in particular.

Most of the time, labels say SALT but sometimes salt appears as SODIUM, which is a part of salt.

How much is a lot?

Even if you've read the labels, you still might not know if a food is actually unhealthy. Labels can be misleading. Some products are labelled as low fat, but are very high in other things, such as sugar or salt.

Guideline daily amounts

The amounts of certain things you should eat each day change a little depending on your height, age and sex. But this chart gives you a rough idea. You will often find a similar guideline chart to this printed on food labels.

Each day	age 5-10	11-16
Fat	70g	70g
of which is saturated fat	20g	25g
Sugar	85g	90g
Fibre	15g	20g
Salt	4g	6g

Some food that you might think is good for you can be extremely unhealthy when you take a closer look. For example, breakfast cereals may contain vitamins, iron, whole grains and calcium, which is great – but some may contain a lot of sugar too, so check the packet.

Some cereals can contain as much as 18.5g of sugar per serving, which is nearly a quarter of your guideline daily amount.

Take a closer look

Look at the snacks below. Maybe you won't be so quick to scoff one when you see what's in it.

Crisps usually contain a lot of fat – about 9g per packet.

A can of cola contains 35g of sugar – that's 8 teaspoons per can.

This 62g chocolate bar contains 18g of fat and 35g of sugar.

This breakfast cereal bar contains 3g of fat.

When it comes to fat and salt, ready meals can be one of the most unhealthy things you can buy. Here are some examples of the worst around...

Lasagne
20.7g fat
9.8g saturated fat
2.7g salt
2.6g sugars

Shepherd's pie
25.1g fat
13.4g saturated fat
3.3g sugars
2g salt

Chicken korma with rice
37.5g fat
14g saturated fat
11g sugars
2g salt

But you can eat much healthier home-made versions of the same dishes and be sure that no unnecessary fat, sugar or salt has gone into them.

What's a healthy weight?

It's natural to think about what you look like and even to compare yourself to other people. The important thing to remember is that there are no rules for how people should look, so it's okay to be different.

Body image

Many people feel pressure to look a certain way. It's normal to want to look good, but unrealistic to try to look like a celebrity. Celebrities often look the way they do because they spend vast amounts of time and money on their appearance, and diet and exercise excessively. In any case, not everyone likes the same body types and looks, so it's best to go with what suits you.

Overweight or not?

It's healthy to put on some weight when you are growing up. Your body needs some extra fat to cope with all the changes you'll go through. You might even double your weight between the ages of 9 and 18. But as you grow taller you'll also appear slimmer again.

   If you really think you are overweight, then it's a good idea to talk to your parents, a school nurse or a doctor. Doctors can work out your body mass index (BMI) from your weight, height, age and sex. This will tell you if you need to lose some weight. Doctors can advise you how to lose weight safely.

Dangerous dieting

Some people follow extreme dieting methods – such as eating nothing but cabbage soup or taking slimming pills. This makes people lose weight fast, but it isn't healthy and the loss won't last.

People who go on these kinds of diets are not getting the nutrients they need, and they risk becoming seriously ill. They'll also put the weight back on as soon as they go back to their normal eating habits.

Eating disorders

Eating disorders are serious illnesses triggered by emotional problems, not by food itself. People who have anorexia don't eat enough, because they think they are fat when they are not. Sufferers from bulimia binge eat lots of food, then make themselves vomit for fear of getting fat.

Anyone who may be developing an eating disorder should tell an adult they trust straightaway – the sooner medical treatment starts, the easier it is to recover.

Losing weight

The only good way to lose weight is to eat balanced meals and to exercise regularly. Cutting down on junk food and taking up a sport (see pages 44-45 for ideas) is a good start to a healthier lifestyle.

How to make food healthier

There are lots of easy ways that you can make the food you eat healthier...

Read the labels on processed food, especially cereals and canned foods. Avoid those which have added salt and sugar.

Eat wholemeal bread and pasta and brown rice. They contain more fibre and vitamins and minerals than white versions of the same food.

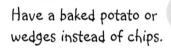

Try to eat more raw vegetables, as they contain more nutrients.

Have a baked potato or wedges instead of chips.

Eat more oily fish, such as salmon or sardines. They contain fats called omega 3s. These can help to prevent heart disease and even make you brainier.

Avoid too many fried foods. Try grilling or stir-frying, which use much less fat.

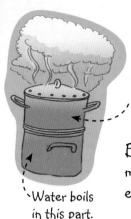

The hot steam in this part cooks the vegetables.

Don't overcook vegetables. Instead of boiling them, try steaming as this keeps in many more of the nutrients.

Water boils in this part.

Buy the low-fat versions of foods such as mayonnaise and creamy salad dressings, especially if you eat a lot of them.

Have yogurt or low-fat crème fraîche instead of cream. You might even find you prefer it.

Drink semi-skimmed milk instead of full-fat. You should drinks lots of milk when you are growing up, as it's good for your bones.

Snack ideas

Instead of a bag of crisps, try these...

* A piece of fruit
* Olives
* Cherry tomatoes
* Mini box of raisins
* Bag of mixed nuts, seeds and fruit – try cashew nuts, walnuts, sunflower or pumpkin seeds and dried fruits such as apricots, raisins and bananas. You could even add a few chocolate drops.
* Yogurt – check the labels to make sure they are low in fat and sugar. Some yogurts are packed with both.
* Unsalted pretzels (they contain less fat than crisps).
* Sticks of raw carrot, pepper or cucumber, or breadsticks, with hummus. (For easy and tasty dip recipes, see page 46.)

33

Life before junk

Junk food wasn't always around. In fact, it's fairly new. Sixty years ago, before there were huge supermarkets and fast-food restaurants, people bought their food from local shops and markets selling it straight from the farm.

Everyone had to make their meals from scratch, because there was little processed food and no ready meals. There was no fast food either, so people couldn't just grab food on the go. But today, junk food is a part of most people's lives.

The obesity issue

Junk food can make some people very fat or even obese. Obesity is a serious health problem that's becoming more and more common. If someone is obese, it means they are so overweight that it could damage their health and even make them die younger.

The problem isn't helped by portion sizes, which are generally bigger these days. And some fast-food restaurants offer supersize helpings at cheap prices.

Not enough exercise

It's not just unhealthy diets that are making people obese. Lots of people aren't doing enough exercise either. Years ago, there were far fewer cars, hardly anyone had a TV, and no one had a computer at home.

People generally used to walk or cycle to school or work...

...but now they often drive.

Household chores were sweaty work...

...but now they're easy!

And everyone spent much more time being energetic outdoors...

...not sitting inside, playing computer games and watching TV.

Energy-saving machines are great, but lots of people don't find other ways to make sure they stay fit. Governments, schools and doctors are campaigning to persuade people to ditch the junk *and* do some exercise.

If it's bad, why buy it?

You might think you are naturally drawn to things in the shops. But there are lots of mysterious powers at work that might have had an effect on what you buy.

The magic of marketing

Marketing is what companies do to make you want to buy something. They might design pretty packaging or exciting adverts so you think it's cool and can't resist buying it.

Marketing can be very useful. It tells people what's available, but it can also be very sneaky – especially when it comes to selling junk food.

Pester power

Chocolate bars and sweets are often just by the till in stores and supermarkets. So, while you're waiting in the queue, your eyes may wander and you may be tempted to reach for just one little bar of chocolate.

The sweet treats are often at the perfect height for tiny, grabbing hands. Parents may get so fed up with their children pestering them that they give in and buy the junk.

Tricks of the trade

There are loads of other ways those cunning marketers get you to buy junk food. Do you recognize any of these?

1. Free toys

Fast-food restaurants often give away free toys with their kids' meals. Do children want to visit the restaurant for the food or the toy?

2. Sports and pop stars

Celebrities sometimes advertise fizzy drinks or junk food. If you like the star, it may encourage you to buy what they're selling.

3. The internet

Next time you're surfing the internet, notice how many of the exciting-looking sites for kids have links to junk food.

4. Buy one, get one free

But it's a bargain! It may well be cheap, but those crafty marketers have got you buying double the amount of unhealthy food.

5. Cartoon characters

Using popular characters from television is an old classic. If kids love something on TV, chances are they'll want the snacks that have the characters' pictures on them.

Food for thought

There can be more to shopping than just picking up a packet of something and buying it. Do you know how your food got from the field to your shopping trolley?

Food miles

The distance food has travelled to get to your plate is sometimes described as food miles – and it can travel a very, very long way. People have got used to having food from all over the world, all the year round.

Environmental campaigners are worried about the huge amounts of fuel burned by planes and trucks on long journeys. Vehicles use up precious energy resources as well as causing pollution and adding to global warming.

Buy local, in season

Lots of foods, such as pineapples or rice, can only be grown in certain parts of the world. And some things, such as strawberries, may be grown near you, but only at certain times of the year. It's a good idea to buy food that's in season locally instead of food that has come a long way. It will be fresher and contain more nutrients, as well as having travelled fewer food miles.

In supermarkets you can find out where food has come from by looking at the packaging.

Fairtrade

Many small-scale farmers in poorer, developing countries don't get paid enough for the products they sell to richer countries. Fairtrade products are marked with a logo which shows that the farmers have been paid fairly.

Look for Fairtrade logos on products such as coffee, tea, bananas and chocolate.

Animal welfare

Some people won't buy meat because of the way the animals are farmed. Many animals are kept in poor conditions without enough fresh air, or they're transported long distances in cramped containers. If you buy free-range meat or eggs, it is more likely that the animals have been treated well and it will probably taste better too.

Fish at risk

Overfishing means that if large numbers of one kind of fish are caught, the species could die out. The fish don't have a chance to mate and reproduce before they're caught.

Other sea life is dying out because of fishing equipment. Trawl fishing drags nets along the seabed, picking up and killing lots of other wildlife along with the fish it's catching.

Some fishermen will only use methods that don't threaten sealife. This is known as sustainable fishing. It will say on seafood packaging if these methods have been used.

How food is grown

There are many different ways
to grow food and people don't
always agree about them...

What does GM mean?

GM stands for genetically modified. It
describes plants that have been changed –
or modified – to grow in a different way.
Scientists modify the plants' genes – the
things which control how a living thing
looks and grows.

Here are some reasons they do it:

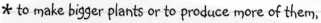

* to make bigger plants or to produce more of them,
* so that the plants don't go off - or rot - as quickly,
* so that the plants won't be damaged by certain herbicides that
  are sprayed on them to kill weeds.

Soya is often
genetically modified.
These foods may
contain GM soya.

Lots of people think genetic modification is
a great way to make food exactly as we
want it. In the future, it may even help poor
countries grow crops in dry or salty soil.

But others worry that scientists have gone
too far. They say they are interfering with
nature and that we don't know what the
long-term effects will be. Some scientists want
to experiment with animals' genes for GM
food. But so many people are against it that
so far it hasn't been allowed.

What does organic mean?

Organic farmers and manufacturers grow and produce food in the most natural way possible. They don't use any artificial chemical fertilizers to help their plants grow, or pesticides to kill pests. The reason is that they think the chemicals in them are dangerous for farm workers, and damage the environment and wildlife. Organic farmers don't grow GM crops, as they're not natural either.

Animals reared for organic meat have better living conditions and are not fed on any artificial chemicals. Organic processed foods, such as bread or pasta, are prepared without any artificial chemicals or additives.

But is it better?

Most people agree that organic food is better because it doesn't use chemicals that are harmful to wildlife. Some people also think it might be better for you too, because you don't eat any of the chemicals that get left on the non-organic food.

People who buy organic food think it tastes better and has higher levels of vitamins and minerals. It may be tastier, but there is no proof that it is nutritionally better for you. Lots of people don't buy organic food because it is often more expensive and harder to find.

Fitness and food

Everybody needs to do some exercise to keep healthy. It is good for your heart and muscles, and for keeping your joints flexible.

It also makes you feel more energetic, reduces stress and helps you stay at a healthy weight.

What to eat before exercise

You don't need to eat anything special before you exercise. Starchy foods, such as a sandwich or pasta dish, are great because they contain carbohydrates which release energy gradually into your bloodstream. If you eat something like this an hour or two before you exercise, it will help to keep you going. Don't eat too close to exercising though, or you will feel sluggish and might get indigestion or cramp.

You will probably be hungry after you've exercised, so make sure you eat then to recharge your batteries.

What about sports foods and drinks?

Sports drinks and energy bars are designed to give athletes a quick boost. They are high in energy, often because they are high in sugar or fat. Lots of energy drinks contain as much sugar as a can of cola.

Professional athletes may use these, but only because they burn huge amounts of energy through very intense activity.

But you won't need them, if you have eaten properly beforehand. You might need a snack though. Bananas are a fantastic choice as they contain natural fruit sugars and lots of energy.

Drink up

It's a good idea to try to drink plenty of water during the day. But you should drink even more when you exercise because you sweat more, which means your body loses water. Drink lots so that you don't get dehydrated. If you have a dry mouth, feel thirsty or have a headache, drink some more water.

Find your sport

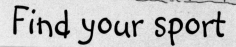

There are so many ways to keep fit, there's bound to be something you'll enjoy. And if you choose an activity to do with a friend, it'll be more fun.

Safety first

To prevent injury, always wear the right clothes and have the correct sports equipment.

How much exercise do I need?

Doctors say you should do an hour of exercise a day. It doesn't have to be a sport – anything that gets your heart beating faster will do. Walking briskly to school, running around with your friends, dancing to the radio, and even helping with housework and gardening, all count.

Some ideas...

With a friend

* Rollerblading
* Jogging
* Skateboarding
* Ice-skating
* Skipping
* Cycling — always wear a helmet and have working lights and reflective clothing for dark days.
* Walking — the faster the better

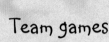

Team games

* Football
* Cricket
* Netball
* Volleyball
* Hockey
* Lacrosse
* Basketball
* Rugby

Indoor activities

* Trampolining
* Aerobics
* Dancing
* Gymnastics
* Martial arts (e.g. karate, judo)
* Table tennis

Racket games

* Tennis
* Squash
* Badminton
* Racketball

Water sports

* Swimming
* Water volleyball
* Water polo
* Water aerobics

* Surfing
* Water-skiing
* Windsurfing

Healthy snacks

These dips are easy to make and a delicious snack to share with your friends. Cut raw vegetables, such as carrots, cucumber, celery or peppers, into strips and dip away.

Guacamole

2 ripe avocados
Juice of half a lemon
1 crushed clove of garlic
4 ripe juicy tomatoes

Scoop out the avocados into a bowl. Add the lemon juice and garlic. Use a fork to mash the avocados until they are smooth. Then, cut the tomatoes into small pieces and mix them in.

Spicy salsa

6 ripe juicy tomatoes
2 spring onions
2 tablespoons fresh
   coriander
Juice of one lime
1-2 drops of hot
   pepper sauce

Chop the tomatoes into very small pieces and put them into a bowl. Add the onions and coriander, both finely chopped.
Then mix in the lime juice and pepper sauce.

Hummus

400g (14oz) can chickpeas
Juice of half a lemon
1 crushed clove of garlic
½ teaspoon ground cumin
2 tablespoons olive oil
150ml (¼ pint) fromage frais
Salt and pepper

Drain the chickpeas and rinse them under cold water. Put them in a bowl and add the lemon juice, garlic, cumin, olive oil, fromage frais and a pinch of salt and pepper. Use an electric or hand-held blender to blend the mixture until it's smooth.

Glossary of food words

additive – a natural or artificial chemical added to food.

carbohydrates – found in bread, potatoes, rice, pasta and cereals.

Fairtrade – Fairtrade products ensure that farmers are paid fairly for their produce.

fibre – found in vegetables, fruit, wholemeal bread and pasta, whole grain cereals, brown rice, beans and nuts.

food miles – the distance food travels from the farm where it was grown to your plate.

genetically modified (GM) – used to describe plants that have had their genes changed to grow in a different way.

guideline daily amounts (GDA) – the recommended amount of something you should eat each day.

hydrogenated fat – an unnatural fat produced when making processed food.

kilojoules (kj) or kilocalories (kcal) – the energy food gives you is measured in these.

organic – grown or reared in the most natural way possible.

preservatives – additives that make food last for longer.

processed food – food made or put together in a factory.

protein – found in meat, fish, eggs, nuts, beans and lentils.

ready meals – processed meals, often high in fat and salt.

saturated fat – the type of fat in meat and dairy products.

Internet links

For links to websites where you can find out more about junk food, go to the Usborne Quicklinks Website at www.usborne-quicklinks.com and type the keywords junk food. The recommended websites are regularly reviewed and updated but, please note, Usborne Publishing is not responsible for the content of websites other than its own.

Index

Photographic manipulation by Nick Wakeford